NATIONAL STRATEGY FOR TRUSTED IDENTITIES IN CYBERSPACE

Enhancing Online Choice, Efficiency, Security, and Privacy

APRIL 2011

THE WHITE HOUSE
WASHINGTON

THE WHITE HOUSE
WASHINGTON

The Internet has transformed how we do business, opening up markets and connecting our economy as never before. It has revolutionized the ways in which we communicate with one another, whether with a friend down the street or a colleague across the globe. And as we have seen in recent weeks, it has empowered people all over the world with tools to share information and speak their minds. In short, the growth of the Internet has been one of the greatest forces for innovation and progress in history.

That is why we are strengthening our communications infrastructure. That is why we are making it easier for the private sector to expand wireless broadband across America. And that is why I am outlining a strategy to make online transactions more secure for businesses and consumers alike: the National Strategy for Trusted Identities in Cyberspace.

The rapid and vastly positive changes that have followed the rise of online transactions – like making purchases or downloading bank statements – have also led to new challenges. Few have been as costly or nerve wracking for businesses and families as online fraud and identity theft. These crimes cost companies and individuals billions of dollars each year; and they often leave in their wake a mess of ruined credit and damaged finances that can take years to repair. But there are other costs for our economy that are more difficult to measure. The potential for fraud and the weakness of privacy protections often leave individuals, businesses, and government reluctant to conduct major transactions online. For example, providing patients with access to their medical records from their home computers requires that hospitals be able to confidently identify that patient online.

Giving consumers choices for solving these kinds of problems is at the heart of this new strategy. And it is one that relies not on government, but on the private sector to design the technologies and tools that will help make our identities more secure in cyberspace and to make those tools available to consumers who want them. It asks companies to pursue these solutions in ways that will not impinge on the vitality and dynamism of the web, or force anyone to give up the anonymity they enjoy on the Internet.

The simple fact is, we cannot know what companies have not been launched, what products or services have not been developed, or what innovations are held back by the inadequacy of tools, like insecure passwords, long ago overwhelmed by the fantastic and unpredictable growth of the Internet. What we do know is this: by making online transactions more trustworthy and enhancing consumers' privacy, we will prevent costly crime; we will give businesses and consumers new confidence; and we will foster growth and innovation, online and across our economy – in some ways we can predict, and in other ways we can scarcely imagine. Ultimately, that is the goal of this strategy.

Table of Contents

Executive Summary

A secure cyberspace is critical to our prosperity.[1] We use the Internet and other online environments to increase our productivity, as a platform for innovation, and as a venue in which to create new businesses. "Our digital infrastructure, therefore, is a strategic national asset, and protecting it—while safeguarding privacy and civil liberties—is a national security priority" and an economic necessity.[2] By addressing threats in this environment, we will help individuals protect themselves in cyberspace and enable both the private sector and government to offer more services online.

As a Nation, we are addressing many of the technical and policy shortcomings that have led to insecurity in cyberspace. Among these shortcomings is the online authentication of people and devices: the President's Cyberspace Policy Review established trusted identities as a cornerstone of improved cybersecurity.[3]

In the current online environment, individuals are asked to maintain dozens of different usernames and passwords, one for each website with which they interact. The complexity of this approach is a burden to individuals, and it encourages behavior—like the reuse of passwords—that makes online fraud and identity theft easier. At the same time, online businesses are faced with ever-increasing costs for managing customer accounts, the consequences of online fraud, and the loss of business that results from individuals' unwillingness to create yet another account. Moreover, both businesses and governments are unable to offer many services online, because they cannot effectively identify the individuals with whom they interact. Spoofed websites, stolen passwords, and compromised accounts are all symptoms of inadequate authentication mechanisms.

Just as there is a need for methods to reliably authenticate individuals, there are many Internet transactions for which identification and authentication is not needed, or the information needed is limited. It is vital to maintain the capacity for anonymity and pseudonymity in Internet transactions in order to enhance individuals' privacy and otherwise support civil liberties. Nonetheless, individuals and businesses need to be able to check each other's identity for certain types of sensitive transactions, such as online banking or accessing electronic health records.

The *National Strategy for Trusted Identities in Cyberspace* (NSTIC or Strategy) charts a course for the public and private sectors to collaborate to raise the level of trust associated with the identities of individuals, organizations, networks, services, and devices involved in online transactions.

---

1. Cyberspace is the interdependent network of information technology components that underpins many of our communications; the Internet is one component of cyberspace.

2. "National Security Strategy." The White House. May 2010, p. 27. Web. 17 Dec. 2010. http://www.whitehouse.gov/sites/default/files/rss_viewer/national_security_strategy.pdf

3. "Cyberspace Policy Review: Assuring a Trusted and Resilient Information and Communications Infrastructure." The White House. May 2009, p. 33. Web. 2 Jun. 2010. http://www.whitehouse.gov/assets/documents/Cyberspace_Policy_Review_final.pdf.

The Strategy's vision is:

Individuals and organizations utilize secure, efficient, easy-to-use, and interoperable identity solutions to access online services in a manner that promotes confidence, privacy, choice, and innovation.

The realization of this vision is the user-centric "Identity Ecosystem" described in this Strategy. It is an online environment where individuals and organizations will be able to trust each other because they follow agreed upon standards to obtain and authenticate their digital identities—and the digital identities of devices. The Identity Ecosystem is designed to securely support transactions that range from anonymous to fully-authenticated and from low- to high-value. The Identity Ecosystem, as envisioned here, will increase the following:

- **Privacy protections** for individuals, who will be able trust that their personal data is handled fairly and transparently;
- **Convenience** for individuals, who may choose to manage fewer passwords or accounts than they do today;
- **Efficiency** for organizations, which will benefit from a reduction in paper-based and account management processes;
- **Ease-of-use**, by automating identity solutions whenever possible and basing them on technology that is simple to operate;
- **Security**, by making it more difficult for criminals to compromise online transactions;
- **Confidence** that digital identities are adequately protected, thereby promoting the use of online services;
- **Innovation**, by lowering the risk associated with sensitive services and by enabling service providers to develop or expand their online presence;
- **Choice**, as service providers offer individuals different—yet interoperable—identity credentials and media.

Examples that illustrate some potential benefits of the Identity Ecosystem can be found throughout the Strategy within the "Envision It!" callout boxes.

The enhancement of privacy and support of civil liberties is a guiding principle of the envisioned Identity Ecosystem. The Identity Ecosystem will use privacy-enhancing technology and policies to inhibit the ability of service providers to link an individual's transactions, thus ensuring that no one service provider can gain a complete picture of an individual's life in cyberspace. By default, only the minimum necessary information will be shared in a transaction. For example, the Identity Ecosystem will allow a consumer to provide her age during a transaction without also providing her birth date, name, address, or other identifying data.

In addition to privacy protections, the Identity Ecosystem will preserve online anonymity and pseudonymity, including anonymous browsing. These efforts to enhance privacy and otherwise support civil liberties will be part of, and informed by, broader privacy policy development efforts occurring throughout the Administration. Equally important, participation in the Identity Ecosystem will be voluntary: the government will neither mandate that individuals obtain an Identity Ecosystem credential nor that companies require Identity Ecosystem credentials from consumers as the only means to interact with them.

The second guiding principle is that identity solutions must be secure and resilient. Trusted digital identities are only one part of layered security, and online security will not be achieved through the establishment of an Identity Ecosystem alone. However, more secure identification and authentication will both ameliorate existing security failures and provide a critical tool with which to improve other areas of online security. The Identity Ecosystem must therefore continue to develop in parallel with ongoing national efforts to improve platform, network, and software security—and efforts to raise awareness of the steps, both technical and non-technical, that individuals and organizations can take to improve their security.

The third guiding principle of the Identity Ecosystem is to ensure policy and technology interoperability among identity solutions, which will enable individuals to choose between and manage multiple different interoperable credentials. Interoperability will also support identity portability and will enable service providers within the Identity Ecosystem to accept a variety of credential and identification media types.

The fourth guiding principal is that the Identity Ecosystem must be built from identity solutions that are cost-effective and easy to use. History and common sense tell us that privacy and security technology is most effective when it exhibits both of these characteristics.

The Strategy will only be a success—and the ideal of the Identity Ecosystem will only be fulfilled—if the guiding principles of privacy, security, interoperability, and ease-of-use are achieved. Achieving them separately will not only lead to an inadequate solution but could serve as a hindrance to the broader evolution of cyberspace. Specifically, achieving interoperability without the appropriate security and privacy measures could encourage abuses of personal and proprietary information beyond those that occur today. However, this risk is more likely to be realized if we take no action: identity solutions in cyberspace are already evolving. One key role for the Federal Government in the implementation of this Strategy is to partner with the private sector to ensure that the Identity Ecosystem implements all of the guiding principles. The Federal Government's role is also to coordinate a whole-of-government approach to implementation, including fostering cooperation across all levels of government, to deliver integrated, constituent-centric services.

The Strategy emphasizes that some parts of the Identity Ecosystem exist today but recognizes that there is much work still to be done. The Strategy seeks to promote the existing marketplace, encourage new solutions where none exist, and establish a baseline of privacy, security, interoperability, and ease of use that will enable the market to flourish. Central to the Strategy's approach is the conviction that the role of government in achieving the Identity Ecosystem is critical and must be carefully calibrated. On the one hand, government should not over-define or over-regulate the existing and growing market for identity and authentication services. If government were to choose a single approach to develop the Identity Ecosystem, it could inhibit innovation and limit private-sector opportunities. On the other hand, the current market for interoperable and privacy-enhancing solutions remains fragmented and incomplete, and its pace of evolution does not match the Nation's needs.

The private sector will lead the development and implementation of this Identity Ecosystem, and it will own and operate the vast majority of the services within it. The Identity Ecosystem should be market-driven, and it should provide a foundation for the development of new and innovative services. The Strategy's approach is for the Federal Government to promote the emergence of an integrated landscape of solutions, building on a number of existing or new public and private initiatives to facilitate the creation of the Identity Ecosystem. The role of the Federal Government is to support and enable the private sector; lead by example in utilizing and offering these services; enhance the protection of individuals; and ensure the guiding principles of privacy, security, interoperability, and ease of use are implemented and maintained in the Identity Ecosystem.

The Federal Government is initiating two short-term actions to implement the Strategy. These are to:

- **Develop an Implementation Roadmap** that identifies and assigns responsibility for actions that the Federal Government can perform itself or by which the Federal Government can facilitate private-sector efforts.

- **Establish a National Program Office (NPO)** for coordinating the activities of the Federal Government and its private-sector partners. The NPO will be hosted at the Department of Commerce and accountable to the President, through the Secretary of Commerce.

The complete Identity Ecosystem will take many years to develop, and achieving this vision will require the dedicated efforts of both the public and private sectors. The Federal Government commits to collaborate with the private sector; state, local, tribal, and territorial governments; and international governments–and to provide the support and action necessary to make the Identity Ecosystem a reality. With a concerted, cooperative effort from all of these parties, individuals will realize the benefits of the Identity Ecosystem through the conduct of their daily transactions in cyberspace.

The Way Forward

The National Program Office will continue the national dialog among the private sector, public sector, and individuals on the implementation of the Strategy. Shortly after the release of the Strategy, the NPO will hold a series of meetings to highlight the existing work in this area and to support the private sector's standardization of policies and technology for the Identity Ecosystem.

Representatives from industry, academia, civil society organizations, standards-setting organizations, and all levels of government are encouraged to attend and collaborate on the design of the Identity Ecosystem. Together, we will work towards technology and policy standards that offer greater identity security and convenience; create new commercial opportunities; and promote innovation, choice, and privacy.

Introduction

Imagine a world where individuals can conduct sensitive business transactions online with reduced fear of identity theft or fraud and without the need to manage scores of usernames and passwords. They can seamlessly access information and services from the private sector, other individuals, and the government. When they need to assert their identity online, they can choose from a number of different types of credentials. They can choose to obtain those credentials from a range of different identity providers, both private and public. Individuals can better trust the identities of the entities with which they interact; as a result, they can conduct a wider array of transactions online to save time and effort. All of these activities occur together with enhanced privacy protections that are built into the underlying processes and technologies. At the same time, individuals will retain their existing options of anonymity and pseudonymity in Internet transactions.

In this world, organizations efficiently conduct business online by trusting the identities and credentials provided by other entities. They can eliminate redundant processes associated with managing, authenticating, authorizing, and validating identity data. They can reduce loss due to fraud or data theft, and they can offer additional services previously deemed too risky to conduct online.

A Platform for Security, Privacy, and Innovation

For our Nation to continue to drive economic growth over the Internet, we must provide individuals and organizations the ability and the option to securely identify each other. When individuals and organizations can trust online identities, they can offer and use online services too complex and sensitive to have been otherwise available.

Some of the technologies needed to solve this problem are emerging. For low-assurance transactions, individuals can already choose from a number of private-sector identity providers.[4] Using these services, individuals can use a single username and password to log in to many different websites, and the website trusts a third-party "identity provider" to check the username and password. Although these technologies provide a glimpse of the future, they have not addressed many of the significant shortcomings of the current environment. Most of today's identity providers use relatively weak usernames and passwords, and most individuals are unable to obtain high-assurance credentials with an acceptable level of security, privacy and interoperability. Almost no existing solutions allow individuals to assert their actual identities online, so the government and private sector are unable to offer online versions of many high-value or more sensitive services.

---

4. The level of assurance in a transaction is the degree to which the parties need to know each other's identity. In a low-assurance transaction, you may not need to know exactly who the other party is. For a high assurance transaction, you may want to know their true identity.

Acknowledging this need, the President's Cyberspace Policy Review stated that:

> "The Federal Government—in collaboration with industry and the civil liberties and privacy communities—should build a cybersecurity-based identity management vision and strategy for the Nation that considers an array of approaches, including privacy-enhancing technologies. The Federal Government must interact with citizens through myriad information, services, and benefit programs and thus has an interest in the protection of the public's private information as well."[5]

This Strategy answers that call. An interagency team received vital input from the private sector—through eighteen critical infrastructure/key resource sectors, nearly seventy different non-profits and Federal advisory groups, and a public comment period—to develop the *National Strategy for Trusted Identities in Cyberspace* (NSTIC).

The Federal Government is already seeking to create this world for its own operations by executing the Federal Identity, Credential, and Access Management (FICAM) Roadmap.[6] The Strategy seeks to accelerate those activities and to foster the development of an Identity Ecosystem in which trusted identities are available to any individual or organization.

Motivation

The Nation faces a host of increasingly sophisticated threats to the personal, sensitive, financial, and confidential information of organizations and individuals. Fraudulent transactions within the banking, retail, and other sectors—along with online intrusions into the Nation's critical infrastructure, such as electric utilities—are all too common. As more commercial and government services become available online, the amount of sensitive information transmitted over the Internet will increase. Consequently, the probability of loss associated with data theft, unauthorized modifications, fraud, and privacy breaches will also increase. Although the total amount of losses—both financial and non-financial—due to online fraud and cybercrime is difficult to quantify, the problem is real and it is increasing.[7]

Furthermore, the online environment today is not user-centric. Individuals tend to have little ability to manage their own personal information once it is released to service providers, and they often must calculate the tradeoffs among security, privacy, and gaining access to a service they desire. In addition, individuals have limited ability to use strong digital identities across multiple applications, because

5. "Cyberspace Policy Review: Assuring a Trusted and Resilient Information and Communications Infrastructure." The White House. May 2009, p. 33. Web. 2 Jun. 2010. http://www.whitehouse.gov/assets/documents/Cyberspace_Policy_Review_final.pdf.

6. See "Federal Identity, Credential, and Access Management (FICAM) Roadmap and Implementation Guidance" Federal Chief Information Officers Council and the Federal Enterprise Architecture, Web. 2 Jun. 2010 http://www.idmanagement.gov/documents/FICAM_Roadmap_Implementation_Guidance.pdf.

7. The 2009 Internet Crime Report states, "From January 1, 2009, through December 31, 2009, the Internet Crime Complaint Center (IC3) Web site received 336,655 complaint submissions. This was a 22.3% increase as compared to 2008…the total dollar loss from all referred cases was $559.7 million…up from $264.6 million in 2008. – "2009 Internet Crime Report." Internet Crime Complaint Center. IC3. 12 Mar. 2010, p. 14. Web. 2 Jun. 2010. http://www.ic3.gov/media/annualreport/2009_IC3Report.pdf.

Over 10 million Americans are also victims of identity theft each year. – "The Department of Justice's Efforts to Combat Identity Theft." U.S. Department of Justice. Office of the Inspector General. Mar. 2010. Web. 2 Jun. 2010. http://www.justice.gov/oig/reports/plus/a1021.pdf.

A Federal Trade Commission survey found that some victims of identity theft can spend more than 130 hours reconstructing their identities (e.g., credit rating, bank accounts, reputation, etc.) following an identity crime. – "2006 Identity Theft Survey Report." Federal Trade Commission. Nov. 2007 p. 6. Web. 2 Jun. 2010. http://www.ftc.gov/os/2007/11/SynovateFinalReportIDTheft2006.pdf.

application and service providers do not use a common framework. Instead, they face the increasing complexity and inconvenience associated with managing the large number of usernames, passwords, and other identity credentials required to conduct services online with disparate organizations.

Finally, the collection of identity-related information across multiple providers, coupled with the sharing of personal information through the growth of social media, increases the opportunity for data compromise. For example, the personal data that individuals use as "prompts" to recover lost passwords (mother's maiden name, the name of a first pet, etc.) is often publicly available or easily obtained.

The benefits of a widely-deployed, broadly-adopted Identity Ecosystem are as significant as the drawbacks of continuing along the current path. Widespread fraud, data breaches, and the inefficiencies of authenticating parties to online transactions impose economic losses, diminish trust, and prevent some services from being offered online. These tradeoffs and shortcomings are not necessary; innovative technologies exist that can provide security and privacy protections while simultaneously granting individuals access to services they desire.

---

1. Envision It!

Mary is tired of remembering dozens of user names and passwords, so she obtains a digital credential from her Internet service provider that is stored on a smart card. Now that she has the smart card, she is also willing to conduct more sensitive transactions, like managing her healthcare, online. One morning, she inserts the smart card into her computer, and uses the credential on it to "run" some errands, including:

- Logging in to her bank and obtaining digital cash;

- Buying a sweater at a new online retailer—without having to open an account;

- Signing documents to refinance her mortgage;

- Reading the note her doctor left in her personal health record, in response to the blood sugar statistics she had uploaded the day before;

- Sending an email to confirm dinner with a friend; and

- Checking her day's schedule on her employer's intranet portal.

In just minutes, she is done with her errands and has plenty of time to stop at the local coffee shop on her way to work.

Scope

The Strategy focuses on ways to establish and maintain trusted digital identities, which are critical for improving the security of online transactions. **Online transactions** are electronic communications among two or more parties, connected via networks, systems, and computers. Technology and processes for **identification** (establishing unique digital identities) and **authentication** (verifying the identity of a user, process, or device) are at the forefront of this Strategy. In addition, the Strategy focuses on ways of providing trusted and validated attributes to enable organizations to make decisions about **authorization** (approving or giving consent for access). Identification, authentication, and authorization provide the information and assurances necessary for the parties within a given transaction to trust each other. Individuals, organizations, hardware, networks, and software are all participants in an online transaction; therefore, each of these may be identified, authenticated, and authorized.

The Strategy recognizes that trusted digital identity, authentication and authorization processes are one part of layered security. Improvements in identification and authentication are critical to attaining a trusted online environment; however, they must be combined with other crucial aspects of cybersecurity. They must develop in parallel with ongoing national efforts to improve platform, network, and software security—and to raise awareness of the steps, both technical and non-technical, that individuals and organizations can take to improve their security. While the Strategy does not address these other essential efforts, it anticipates that many co-evolving solutions in these areas will need to use trusted identities and improved authentication if we are to improve the security of cyberspace.

---

2. Envision It!

A power utility remotely manages "Smart Grid" software deployed on an electricity meter.

- Secure authentication between the power company and the meter prevents criminals from deploying fraudulent meters to steal electricity.

- Trusted hardware modules ensure that the hardware and software configurations on the meter are correct.

- The meter validates that instructions and periodic software upgrades actually come from the power company.

Trusted interactions among hardware, software, and organizations reduce the threat of fraudulent activity and the deployment of malware within the Smart Grid.

The identity aspects of securing online transactions are a subset of the overall identity management sphere. The Strategy does not explicitly address identity and trust issues in the offline world; however, offline and online identity solutions can and should complement each other. **Identity proofing** (verifying the identity of an individual) and the quality of identity source documents have a profound impact on establishing trusted digital identities, but the Strategy does not prescribe how these processes and documents need to evolve.

Lastly, the Strategy does not advocate for the establishment of a national identification card or system. Nor does the Strategy seek to circumscribe the ability of individuals to communicate anonymously or pseudonymously, which is vital to protect free speech and freedom of association. Instead, the Strategy seeks to provide to individuals and organizations the option of interoperable and higher-assurance credentials to supplement existing options, like anonymity or pseudonymity.

Public-Private Collaboration

The private sector and all levels of government, working together, can foster both economic prosperity and cybersecurity by overcoming the barriers that inhibit the adoption of more trustworthy identities in cyberspace.[8] Such barriers include:

- Concerns regarding personal privacy;

- Lack of secure, convenient, user-friendly options for authentication and identification;

- Uncertainty regarding the allocation and level of liability for fraud or other failures; and

- The absence of a common framework to help establish trusted identities across a diverse landscape of online transactions and constituents.

To bring this world to fruition, close collaboration between the public and private sectors is crucial.

---

8. In this document, "all levels of government" includes Federal, state, local, tribal, and territorial government.

Guiding Principles

The Strategy specifies four Guiding Principles to which the Identity Ecosystem must adhere:

- Identity solutions will be privacy-enhancing and voluntary

- Identity solutions will be secure and resilient

- Identity solutions will be interoperable

- Identity solutions will be cost-effective and easy to use

These principles form the foundation for all of the Strategy's goals, objectives, and actions. The Strategy will only be a success—and the ideal of the Identity Ecosystem will only be fulfilled—if these Guiding Principles are achieved.

Identity Solutions will be Privacy-Enhancing and Voluntary

> ### 3. Envision It!
>
> Antonio, age thirteen, wants to enter an online chat room that is specifically for adolescents, between the ages of twelve and seventeen. His parents give him permission to get a digital credential from his school. His school also acts as an attribute provider: it validates that he is between the age of twelve and seventeen without actually revealing his name, birth date or any other information about him. The credential employs privacy-enhancing technology to validate Antonio's age without informing the school that he is using the credential. Antonio can speak anonymously but with confidence that the other participants are between the ages of twelve and seventeen.

The offline world has structural barriers that preserve individual privacy by limiting information collection, use, and disclosure to a specific context. For example, consider a driver's license: an individual can use a driver's license to open a bank account, board an airplane, or view an age-restricted movie at the cinema, but the Department of Motor Vehicles does not know every place that accepts driver's licenses as identification. It is also difficult for the bank, the airport, and the movie theater to collaborate and link the transactions together. At the same time, there are aspects of these offline transactions that are not privacy-protective. The movie theater attendant who checks an individual's driver's license needs to know only that the individual is over age 17. But looking at the driver's license reveals extraneous information, such as the individual's address and full date of birth.

Ideally, identity solutions should preserve the positive privacy benefits of offline transactions while mitigating some of the negative privacy aspects. The Fair Information Practice Principles (FIPPs) are the widely accepted framework for evaluating and mitigating privacy impacts. The eight FIPPs are transparency, individual participation, purpose specification, data minimization, use limitation, data quality and integrity, security, and accountability and auditing.[9]

---

9. See Appendix A to this document for details on the Fair Information Practice Principles.

The envisioned Identity Ecosystem will be grounded in a holistic implementation of the FIPPs in order to provide multi-faceted privacy protections. For example, organizations will collect and distribute only the information necessary to the transaction, maintain appropriate safeguards on that information, and be responsive and accountable to individuals' privacy expectations. In circumstances where individuals make choices regarding the use of their data (such as to restrict particular uses), those choices will be automatically applied to all parties with whom that individual interacts. Consistent with the FIPPs-based approach, the Identity Ecosystem will include limits on the length of time organizations can retain personal information and will require them to provide individuals with appropriate opportunities to access, correct, and delete it. The Identity Ecosystem will also require organizations to maintain auditable records regarding the use and protection of personal information.

Moreover, a FIPPs-based approach will promote the creation and adoption of privacy-enhancing technical standards. Such standards will minimize the transmission of unnecessary information and eliminate the superfluous "leakage" of information that can be invisibly collected by third parties. Such standards will also minimize the ability to link credential use among multiple service providers, thereby preventing them from developing a complete picture of an individual's activities online. Finally, service providers will request individuals' credentials only when necessary for the transaction and then only as appropriate to the risk associated with the transaction. As a result, implementation of the FIPPs will protect individuals' capacity to engage anonymously in cyberspace. Universal adoption of the FIPPs in the envisioned Identity Ecosystem will enable a variety of transactions, including anonymous, anonymous with validated attributes, pseudonymous, and uniquely identified—while providing robust privacy protections that promote usability and trust.

Finally, participation in the Identity Ecosystem will be voluntary: the government will neither mandate that individuals obtain an Identity Ecosystem credential nor that companies require Identity Ecosystem credentials from consumers as the only means to interact with them. Individuals shall be free to use an Identity Ecosystem credential of their choice, provided the credential meets the minimum risk requirements of the relying party, or to use any non-Identity Ecosystem mechanism provided by the relying party. Individuals' participation in the Identity Ecosystem will be a day-to-day—or even a transaction-to-transaction—choice.

Identity Solutions will be Secure and Resilient

Identity solutions and the processes and techniques used to establish trust must be secure against attack or misuse. Security ensures the confidentiality, integrity, and availability of identity solutions and, when appropriate, the non-repudiation of transactions. The use of open and collaboratively developed security standards and the presence of auditable security processes are critical to an identity solution's trustworthiness. Identity solutions must have security built into them so that whenever possible, the security is transparent to the user.

Identity solutions will provide secure and reliable methods of electronic authentication. Authentication credentials are secure when they are (a) issued based on sound criteria for verifying the identity of individuals and devices; (b) resistant to theft, tampering, counterfeiting, and exploitation; and (c) issued only by providers who fulfill the necessary requirements. In addition, the ability to support robust forensic capabilities will maximize recovery efforts, enable enhancements to protect against evolving threats, and permit attribution, when appropriate, to ensure that criminals can be held accountable for their activities.

Reliable identity solutions will also be available and resilient. Identity solutions are available when they meet appropriate service-level requirements agreed upon by the individuals and organizations that use them. Credentials are resilient when they can recover from loss, compromise, theft—and can be effectively revoked or suspended in instances of misuse. Another contributor to resilience is the existence of a diverse and heterogeneous environment of providers and methods of authentication. In a diverse ecosystem, a participant can easily switch providers if their existing provider becomes insolvent, incapable of adhering to policies, or revises their terms of service. Identity solutions must detect when trust has been broken, be capable of timely restoration after any disruption, be able to quickly revoke and recover compromised digital identities, and be capable of adapting to the dynamic nature of technology.

Identity Solutions will be Interoperable

Interoperability encourages service providers to accept a variety of credential and identity media, similar to the way ATMs accept credit and debit cards from different banks. Interoperability also supports identity portability: it enables individuals to use a variety of credentials in asserting their digital identity to a service provider. Finally, the interoperability of identity solutions envisioned in this Strategy will enable individuals to easily switch providers, thus harnessing market incentives to meet individuals' expectations.

This guiding principle recognizes two interoperability ideals within the Identity Ecosystem:

- There will be standardized, reliable credentials and identity media in widespread use in both the public and private sectors; and

- If an individual, device, or system presents a valid and appropriate credential, any qualified relying party is capable of accepting and verifying the credential as proof of identity and attributes.

To achieve these ideals, identity solutions should be scalable across multiple communities, spanning traditional geographic borders. Interoperable identity solutions will allow organizations to accept and trust external users authenticated by a third party. Identity solutions achieve scalability when all participants in the various identity federations agree upon a common set of standards, requirements, and accountability mechanisms for securely exchanging digital identity information, resulting in authentication across identity federations.

Identity solutions will achieve at least two types of interoperability: technical and policy-level. Technical interoperability (including semantic interoperability) refers to the ability for different technologies to communicate and exchange data based upon well-defined and testable interface standards. Policy-level interoperability is the ability for organizations to adopt common business policies and processes (e.g., liability, identity proofing, and vetting) related to the transmission, receipt, and acceptance of data between systems.

There are many existing standards and standards organizations that address these issues, and the Identity Ecosystem will encourage the use of existing, non-proprietary solutions. When new standards are needed, the Identity Ecosystem will emphasize non-proprietary, international, and industry-led standards. In addition, identity solutions will be modular, allowing service providers to build sophisticated identity systems using smaller and simpler sub-systems. This implementation philosophy will improve the flexibility, reliability, and reuse of these systems, and it will allow for simplicity and efficiency in change management: service providers can add and remove components as the Identity Ecosystem evolves.

Identity Solutions will be Cost-Effective and Easy To Use

From the individual's perspective, the increasing complexity and risk of managing multiple credentials threaten the convenience associated with online transactions.

> ### 4. Envision It!
>
> Parvati uses a credential, issued by a third party and bound to her existing cell phone, to access online government tax services. She can log in with the click of a button: she no longer has to remember the complicated password she previously had to use. She views her tax history, changes her demographic information, files her taxes electronically, and monitors her refund status.

The Identity Ecosystem will promote identity solutions that foster the reduction and elimination of policy and technology silos that require individuals to maintain multiple identity credentials. Individuals will be able to establish a small number of identity credentials that they can leverage across a wide variety of service providers. Organizations will no longer have to issue and maintain credentials for each of their users.

Individuals, businesses, organizations, and all levels of government will benefit from the reduced cost of online transactions: fewer redundant account procedures, a reduction in fraud, decreased help-desk costs, and a transition away from expensive paper-based processes. Furthermore, reusable identity solutions promote operational efficiency and will further reduce the cost of implementing online services. The use of existing identity solutions that align with the Strategy is one way of quickly achieving these efficiencies.

Identity solutions should be simple to understand, intuitive, easy-to-use, and enabled by technology that requires minimal user training. Many existing technology components in widespread use today, such as cell phones, smart cards, and personal computers, can be leveraged to act as or contain a credential. Whenever possible, identity solutions should be built into online services to enhance their usability. Identity solutions must also bridge the 'digital divide'; they must be available to all individuals, and they must be accessible to the disadvantaged and disabled.

Vision

Consistent with the Guiding Principles, the vision of the National Strategy for Trusted Identities in Cyberspace is:

Individuals and organizations utilize secure, efficient, easy-to-use and interoperable identity solutions to access online services in a manner that promotes confidence, privacy, choice, and innovation.

The vision applies to individuals, businesses, non-profits, advocacy groups, associations, and governments at all levels. It cannot be accomplished without the close cooperation between the public and private sectors. It also reflects the user-centric nature of the Identity Ecosystem, which provides greater transparency, privacy protection, flexibility, and choice to the individual.

Working from this collectively developed vision, the remainder of the Strategy plots the journey the Nation must undertake—led by the private sector and enabled by all levels of government—to attain an operational Identity Ecosystem.

Benefits

The benefits of the envisioned Identity Ecosystem for individuals, the private sector, and governments are closely intertwined. Nevertheless, each experiences the benefits of the Identity Ecosystem through the lens of its particular interests and concerns.

Benefits for Individuals

- **Convenience.** Individuals will be able to conduct their personal business online with less time and effort. They will be able to access services easily without having to manage many different usernames and passwords.

- **Privacy.** Individuals' privacy will be enhanced. The Identity Ecosystem will limit the amount of identifying information that is collected and transmitted in the course of online transactions. It will also protect individuals from those who would link individuals' transactions in order to track individuals' online activities.

- **Security.** Individuals can work and play online with fewer concerns about identity theft. Stronger authentication will limit unauthorized transactions, and decreasing the transmission of identifying information will result in less risk from data breaches.

> **5. Envision It!**
>
> Ann learns that her recently issued bank card and her new university card are both Identity Ecosystem-approved credentials. She also discovers that her email provider and social networking site accept both of these credentials, while her health care provider and local utility companies accept the higher assurance bank card. Ann decides to log in to her email and social networking site using her university card, but uses her bank card to log in to her health and utility services. Now she no longer has to remember tens of different usernames and passwords and can conduct different risk transactions with appropriate levels of authentication, all without having to obtain an additional credential.

Benefits for the Private Sector

- **Innovation.** The Identity Ecosystem will provide a platform on which new or more efficient business models will be developed—just as the Internet itself has been a platform for innovation. The Identity Ecosystem will enable new forms of online alliances and co-branding. It will also enable organizations to put new services online, especially for sectors such as healthcare and banking. Early adopters can leverage innovative solutions within the Identity Ecosystem to differentiate their brands in the marketplace.

- **Efficiency.** Online transactions will be practical in more situations. The private sector will have lower barriers to customer enrollment, increased productivity, and decreased costs. Cross-organizational trust will provide businesses with exposure to a large population of potential customers they might not otherwise reach. Not only is there potential access to new customers, the traditional barriers associated with customer enrollment can be eliminated, reducing a friction that prevents potential customers from using a service. The consistency and accuracy of trusted digital identities will improve productivity by, for example, reducing paper-based processes and the help-desk costs associated with account management and password maintenance. Losses due to fraud and identity theft will also be reduced.

- **Trust.** Trusted digital identities will allow organizations to better display and protect their brands online. Participants in the Identity Ecosystem will also be more trusted, because they will have agreed to the Identity Ecosystem's minimum standards for privacy and security.

---

6. Envision It!

A small business wants to start an online store. It decides that participating in the Identity Ecosystem will eliminate the need to develop costly account management features. Moreover, the effort required for a potential customer to establish an account at the store will be decreased—in many cases customers will not need to establish an account at all in order to make a purchase.

The business wants the full benefits of the Identity Ecosystem, so it meets the published, transparent requirements and receives a "trustmark." Customers can see that trustmark and know that the business complies with the policies of the Identity Ecosystem.

The business then selects three types of credentials that meet its security requirements. There are twelve identity providers that meet the businesses requirements, and they have issued a total of thirty million credentials.

As a result, the business immediately has a base of millions of potential customers who can safely and easily shop at the online store without enduring the inconvenience of manually entering information to create an account.

Benefits for Government

- **Constituent Satisfaction.** The Identity Ecosystem will enable government to expand its online services in order to serve its constituents more efficiently and transparently (while still offering in-person services for those who prefer them). It will also enable increased integration among government service providers to coordinate and deliver services to constituents. Technology initiatives, such as the Smart Grid and Health Information Technology, can leverage the capabilities of the Identity Ecosystem to increase participation in the initiative.

- **Economic Growth.** Government support of the Identity Ecosystem will generate innovation in the marketplace that will create new business opportunities and advance U.S. business goals in international trade.

- **Public Safety.** Increasing online security will reduce cyber crime, improve the integrity of networks and systems, and raise overall consumer safety levels. Enhanced online trust will also provide a platform to support more effective and adaptable response to national emergencies.

The benefits just highlighted—and those that will develop over time—will result not from any single component of the Identity Ecosystem but from the emergence of the Identity Ecosystem as a new national platform.

---

7. Envision It!

A large national emergency erupts on the coastline and a call for support results in an influx of first responders at the emergency site.

A federal agency is tracking the event using their global satellite network, and can share detailed information to state and local officials, utility providers, and emergency first responders from all over the country. Each participant in the information exchange uses an interoperable credential issued by his employer to log into the information-sharing portal. The portal automatically directs responders to information relevant to them based on their duties and affiliated organization.

Joel, a doctor, logs in and sees the triage report with injury lists at each of the local emergency shelters. The hospital where he is a resident acts as the attribute provider to verify his status as a doctor and his specialty. The portal indicates that his specialty is in high demand at a center half a mile away, where there is a long waiting time for care.

In addition, Joel accesses an application on his registered cell phone to track changing local conditions. It warns him that two bridges in his area have recently been reported as unsafe and one intersection should be avoided. Joel uses this information to safely navigate to the center where he can be authenticated as a licensed specialist and can most help the victims of the emergency.

The Identity Ecosystem

The Identity Ecosystem is the embodiment of the vision. It is an online environment where individuals and organizations can trust each other because they follow agreed-upon standards and processes to identify and authenticate their digital identities—and the digital identities of organizations and devices. Similar to ecosystems that exist in nature, it will require disparate organizations and individuals to function together and fulfill unique roles and responsibilities, with an overarching set of standards and rules. The Identity Ecosystem will offer, but will not mandate, stronger identification and authentication while protecting privacy by limiting the amount of information that individuals must disclose.

Participating in the Identity Ecosystem

The Identity Ecosystem consists of the participants, policies, processes, and technologies required for trusted *identification, authentication,* and *authorization* across diverse transaction types. The entities and roles described below are part of the Identity Ecosystem. All of the roles may be held by public or private-sector organizations or a combination of both, and a single organization may provide services that cross multiple roles.

Identity Ecosystem Execution Components

- An **individual** is a person engaged in an online transaction. Individuals are the first priority of the Strategy.

- A **non-person entity (NPE)** may also require authentication in the Identity Ecosystem. NPEs can be organizations, hardware, networks, software, or services and are treated much like individuals within the Identity Ecosystem. NPEs may engage in or support a transaction.

- The **subject** of a transaction may be an individual or an NPE.

- **Attributes** are a named quality or characteristic inherent in or ascribed to someone or something (for example, "this individual's age is at least 21 years").

- A **digital identity** is a set of attributes that represent a subject in an online transaction.

- An **identity provider (IDP)** is responsible for establishing, maintaining, and securing the digital identity associated with that subject. These processes include revoking, suspending, and restoring the subject's digital identity if necessary.

- The identity provider may also verify the identity of and sign up (enroll) a subject. Alternatively, verification and enrollment may be performed by a separate **enrolling agent**.

- IDPs issue **credentials**, the information objects used during a transaction to provide evidence of the subject's identity. The credential may also provide a link to the subject's authority, roles, rights, privileges, and other attributes.

- The credential can be stored on an **identity medium**: a device or object (physical or virtual) used for storing one or more credentials, claims, or attributes related to a subject. Identity media are available in many formats, such as smart cards, security chips embedded in personal computers, cell phones, software based certificates, and Universal Serial Bus (USB) devices. Selecting the appropriate identity medium and credential type is implementation-specific and depends on the risk tolerance of the participating entities.

- A **relying party (RP)** makes transaction decisions based upon its receipt, validation, and acceptance of a subject's authenticated credentials and attributes. Within the Identity Ecosystem, a relying party selects and trusts the identity and attribute providers of their choice, based on risk and functional requirements. Relying parties are not required to integrate with all permutations of credential types and identity media. Rather, they can trust an identity provider's assertion of a valid subject credential, as appropriate. Relying parties also typically need to identify and authenticate themselves to the subject as part of transactions in the Identity Ecosystem. Relying parties can choose the strength of the authentication and attributes required to access their services.

- An **attribute provider (AP)** is responsible for the processes associated with establishing and maintaining identity attributes. Attribute maintenance includes validating, updating, and revoking the attribute claim. An attribute provider asserts trusted, validated attribute claims in response to attribute requests from relying parties. In certain instances, a subject may self-assert attribute claims to relying parties. Trusted, validated attributes inform relying parties' decision to authorize subjects.

- **Participants** refer to the collective subjects, identity providers, attribute providers, relying parties and identity media taking part in a given transaction.

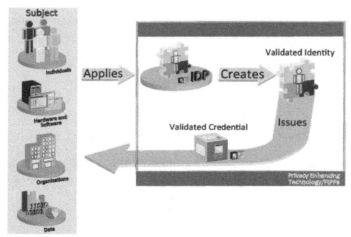

Figure 1: A subject obtains a validated credential to use in online transactions

- A **trustmark** is used to indicate that a product or service provider has met the requirements of the Identity Ecosystem, as determined by an accreditation authority. The trustmark itself, and the way it is presented, will be resistant to tampering and forgery; participants should be able to both visually and electronically validate its authenticity. The trustmark helps individuals and organizations make informed choices about the Identity Ecosystem-related practices of the service providers and identity media they select.

An Example of the Identity Ecosystem

The following provides a functional example of how individuals and organizations can take advantage of the Identity Ecosystem. The Identity Ecosystem supports many types of interactions and the example in this section is just one way in which the guiding principles of the Strategy are upheld.

As shown in Figure 1, individuals or NPEs acting within the Identity Ecosystem can obtain a pseudonymous or uniquely identified credential from an identity provider before conducting transactions online. For higher levels of assurance, identity providers validate subjects' physical identities and make sure that each digital identity accurately reflects the actual person or NPE. Next, identity providers associate a subject's credential with the subject's digital identity.

Individuals or NPEs can obtain validated attribute claims from attribute providers, as depicted in Figure 2. Attribute providers confirm, bind, assert and issue attribute information about a subject. For example, an attribute claim might assert that an individual is older than age twenty-one.

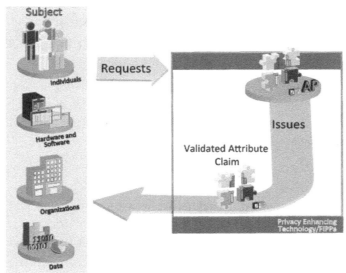

Figure 2: A subject obtains a validated attribute claim to use in online transactions

In Figure 3, the individual or NPE presents credentials and attributes directly to the relying party. The subject uses privacy-enhancing technologies to minimize the information that is revealed to the relying party. The relying party can then validate the credentials and attributes without the need for the identity or attribute providers to know that the subject is performing the transaction. Individuals or NPEs may supply attribute values ("my birth date is March 31, 1974") or verified attribute claims ("I am older than twenty-one") to the relying party. Relying parties are able to authenticate that the credentials and attributes are from valid providers and are current.

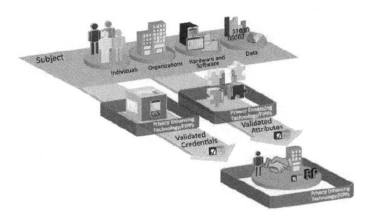

Figure 3: A subject supplies validated credentials and attribute claims to a relying party to authorize an online transaction

Likewise, an individual or NPE is able to make informed choices about relying parties by checking whether or not the relying party has a "trustmark," which certifies that it adheres to the rules of the Identity Ecosystem. When the individual accesses the online services of the relying party, the trustmark is electronically validated.

Consider the situation in which a woman, Keisha, requests medical information from the hospital her husband, John, has recently visited. The hospital requires that any such requests be authenticated using a high assurance credential. In addition, the hospital requires patient approval before releasing personal medical information to other individuals.

Keisha uses the browser on her cell phone to access the hospital website. The browser authenticates the hospital's website domain so that Keisha knows she is not sending information to a fraudulent site. Keisha has a digital certificate issued by her trustmarked cell phone carrier (also her IDP), and the hospital validates the authenticity of the credential, her cell phone, and her digital identity. Next, to receive patient approval for the release of personal records, the hospital obtains validation from John's primary care clinic (the AP). The primary care provider validates and maintains the appropriate attributes in the form of John's approval to release his medical information to Keisha. The hospital uses the clinic's assertion as proof that John digitally signed a medical release authorization form for Keisha, so it allows Keisha to view John's test results. Although all of these operations occur, they happen in the background. All Keisha has to do is browse to the secure website on her credentialed smart phone.

The Policy Foundation of the Identity Ecosystem

The Identity Ecosystem will consist of different online communities that use interoperable technology, processes, and policies. These will be developed over time—but always with a baseline of privacy, interoperability, and security. The different components include:

- The **Identity Ecosystem Framework** is the overarching set of interoperability standards, risk models, privacy and liability policies, requirements, and accountability mechanisms that structure the Identity Ecosystem.

- A **steering group** will administer the process for policy and standards development for the Identity Ecosystem Framework in accordance with the Guiding Principles in this Strategy. The steering group will also ensure that accreditation authorities validate participants' adherence to the requirements of the Identity Ecosystem Framework.

- A **trust framework** is developed by a community whose members have similar goals and perspectives. It defines the rights and responsibilities of that community's participants in the Identity Ecosystem; specifies the policies and standards specific to the community; and defines the community-specific processes and procedures that provide assurance. A trust framework considers the level of risk associated with the transaction types of its participants; for example, for regulated industries, it could incorporate the requirements particular to that industry. Different trust frameworks can exist within the Identity Ecosystem, and sets of participants can tailor trust frameworks to meet their particular needs. In order to be a part of the Identity Ecosystem, all trust frameworks must still meet the baseline standards established by the Identity Ecosystem Framework.

- An **accreditation authority** assesses and validates identity providers, attribute providers, relying parties, and identity media, ensuring that they all adhere to an agreed-upon trust framework. Accreditation authorities can issue trustmarks to the participants that they validate.

- A **trustmark scheme** is the combination of criteria that is measured to determine service provider compliance with the Identity Ecosystem Framework.

The Identity Ecosystem Framework provides a baseline set of standards and policies that apply to all of the participating trust frameworks. This baseline is more permissive at the lowest levels of assurance, to ensure that it does not serve as an undue barrier to entry, and more detailed at higher levels of assurance, to ensure that participants have adequate protections.

The Identity Ecosystem Framework will not be developed overnight. It will take time for different participants to reach agreement on all of the policy and technical standards necessary to fulfill the Strategy's vision. Initially, the Identity Ecosystem Framework is likely to contain a fairly minimal set of commonly agreed upon standards. The Identity Ecosystem Framework will become more robust over time as participants are able to come to agreement on different standards.

Trust frameworks enable communities to elaborate upon the baseline standards and policies from the Identity Ecosystem Foundation. For example, there may be a trust framework for the identification of computer network cards. As another example, mobile phone providers have specific technical needs. Carriers may thus join a trust framework to enable individuals to authenticate using their cell phones as a credential.

One or more private-sector accreditation authorities may be necessary to implement a trust framework. Accreditation authorities validate identity providers, attribute providers, and relying parties, ensuring that they meet the policies and standards set by the trust framework. Existing private-sector organizations already serve in this role in some sectors and can participate in the Identity Ecosystem if they so choose. A public-private steering group will ensure that accreditation authorities maintain the minimum requirements of the Identity Ecosystem Framework when they issue trustmarks.

Figure 4 illustrates multiple trust frameworks built upon the foundation of the Identity Ecosystem Framework. This baseline ensures underlying interoperability such that credentials can be relied upon even when the participants are in different trust frameworks.

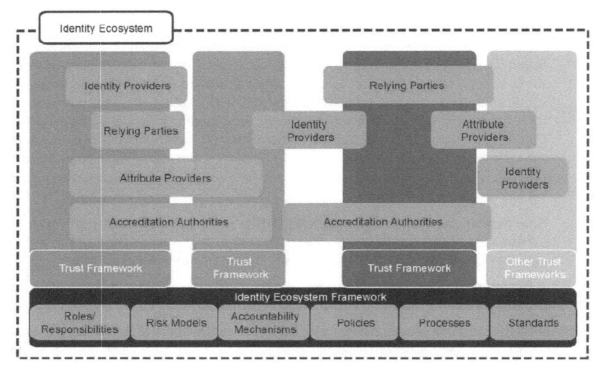

Figure 4: The Identity Ecosystem

The accreditation process and trustmarks can foster trust among all Identity Ecosystem participants. The trustmark is a mechanism for efficiently communicating the policies and technologies that a participant supports. For individuals, the trustmark is a simple alternative to reading documents like terms of service or detailed privacy policies: it can provide an easy means of identifying service providers who abide by a set of uniform policies.

In the hospital example discussed above, trusted relationships exist among Keisha, John, John's hospital, Keisha's cell phone carrier, and John's primary care clinic because they all are part of the Identity Ecosystem. Keisha has the confidence to check John's test results on the hospital website (the RP) because she validates that the hospital, cell phone provider, and primary care physician all have a trustmark, which signifies that they adhere to the Identity Ecosystem Framework.

She knows that she can supply only minimal personal information because the hospital requires only the information necessary to complete the transaction. Privacy enhancing technology enables the cell phone provider to issue a credential that the hospital can validate without contacting the cell phone provider, so Keisha does not leave traces of her online activities for all the participants to aggregate into a complete picture of her life. Under the baseline privacy policies of the Identity Ecosystem Framework, the participants manage and protect the personal information that they do maintain about her.

The accreditation authority validates that the hospital meets the standards of the trust framework (and thus of the Identity Ecosystem Framework). Likewise, the accreditation authority assessed and validated the woman's cell phone carrier as an identity provider, and it validated the physician's clinic as an attribute provider. As a result, the participants in the trust framework could securely and conveniently provide a valued online service to Keisha. The combination of these participants, the standards and agreements between them, and the underlying technologies form the Identity Ecosystem.

Goals and Objectives

In order to fulfill the vision of this Strategy, the Nation must achieve the following goals:

- Develop a comprehensive Identity Ecosystem Framework.

- Build and implement interoperable identity solutions.

- Enhance confidence and willingness to participate in the Identity Ecosystem.

- Ensure the long-term success and viability of the Identity Ecosystem.

The first two goals focus on designing and building the necessary policy and technology to deliver trusted online services. The third goal encourages adoption, including the use of education and awareness efforts. The fourth goal promotes the continued development and enhancement of the Identity Ecosystem. For each goal, there are objectives that enable the achievement of the goal by addressing barriers in the current environment.

These goals will require the active collaboration of all levels of government and the private sector. The private sector will be the primary developer, implementer, owner, and operator of the Identity Ecosystem, which will succeed only if it serves as a platform for innovation in the market. The Federal Government will enable the private sector and will lead by example through the early adoption and provision of Identity Ecosystem services. It will partner with the private sector to develop the Identity Ecosystem, and it will ensure that baseline levels of security, privacy, and interoperability are built into the Identity Ecosystem Framework.

Goal 1: Develop a comprehensive Identity Ecosystem Framework.

The Identity Ecosystem Framework is the overarching set of interoperability standards, risk models, privacy and liability policies, requirements, and accountability mechanisms that govern the Identity Ecosystem. It will guide the development of individual trust frameworks and will be flexible enough to accommodate the varied needs of Identity Ecosystem participants.

Objective 1.1: Establish improved privacy protection mechanisms.

The Identity Ecosystem Framework must offer individuals better means of protecting their privacy by establishing clear rules and guidelines based upon the FIPPs. These rules and guidelines must address not only the circumstances under which a service provider or relying party may share information but also the kinds of information that they may collect and how that information is used. New privacy protections will shift the current model of application-specific collection of identity information to a distributed, user-centric model that supports an individual's capability to manage an array of cyber identities and to manage and assert personal attributes without having to provide identifying data. The new model will reduce the number of service providers with whom individuals must share their personal information in the course of everyday transactions.

The Executive Branch of the Federal Government will work with the private sector and, if necessary, propose legislation to strengthen privacy protections for individuals. These protections will enable individuals to form consistent expectations about the treatment of their information in cyberspace. Although individuals will retain the right to exchange their personal information in return for services they value, these protections will ensure that the default behavior of Identity Ecosystem providers is to:

- Limit the collection and transmission of information to the minimum necessary to fulfill the transaction's purpose and related legal requirements;

- Limit the use of the individual's data that is collected and transmitted to specified purposes;

- Limit the retention of data to the time necessary for providing and administering the services to the individual end-user for which the data was collected, except as otherwise required by law;

- Provide concise, meaningful, timely, and easy-to-understand notice to end-users on how providers collect, use, disseminate, and maintain personal information;

- Minimize data aggregation and linkages across transactions;

- Provide appropriate mechanisms to allow individuals to access, correct, and delete personal information;

- Establish accuracy standards for data used in identity assurance solutions;

- Protect, transfer at the individual's request, and securely destroy information when terminating business operations or overall participation in the Identity Ecosystem;

- Be accountable for how information is actually used and provide mechanisms for compliance, audit, and verification; and

- Provide effective redress mechanisms for, and advocacy on behalf of, individuals who believe their data may have been misused.

Objective 1.2: Establish comprehensive identification and authentication standards based on defined risk models.

Risk models provide a common understanding of the level of assurance required for a type of transaction, based upon the threats to that type of transaction and the potential severity of their impact. For example, the level of authentication required for online banking is likely to differ from that required to access an online magazine subscription. Technical and policy standards based on these risk models will define how to remotely authenticate and manage the digital identities of subjects, including the management of personal information in accordance with privacy laws and best practices.

The Federal Government will facilitate private-sector efforts to establish these risk models and standards in accord with the vision of the Strategy. The effort to develop technical standards should use open, transparent fora and leverage existing, market-recognized guidance on assessing required authentication levels. It should also be informed by and, when possible, seek alignment with international efforts. Both technical and policy standards must enable consistency and interoperability while remaining flexible enough to adapt as security threats evolve and the market innovates. They must also take individual privacy protection into consideration, ensuring that resulting standards have privacy "built in." These technical and policy standards will establish a cross-sector baseline of interoperability and behavior, and they will enhance the confidence of businesses seeking to invest in identity solutions. The ultimate goal of risk-based models and assessment tools will be to support the decisions that organizations make to determine how they will operate within the Identity Ecosystem. Developing standards that cover interoperability requirements, trustmark criteria, and accreditation will pave the way for choice across solutions, ultimately accelerating Identity Ecosystem adoption.

Objective 1.3: Define participant responsibilities in the Identity Ecosystem and establish mechanisms to provide accountability.

The Identity Ecosystem Framework will define the minimum rights and responsibilities of the various participants in the Identity Ecosystem and establish consequences for those that do not uphold their responsibilities. As part of defining these responsibilities, the Identity Ecosystem Framework must establish the accountability and remediation process when an identity credential is fraudulently issued or used or when other breakdowns in the Identity Ecosystem occur. To date, these concerns have been a barrier to the development of widespread identity and authentication solutions at all levels of assurance.

These concerns affect both individuals and service providers. The Identity Ecosystem Framework must in general protect individuals from unbounded liability and in particular ensure that individuals are not held liable for losses that they were powerless to prevent. The Identity Ecosystem Framework should also clarify service provider accountability in order to overcome the uncertainty and fear of unbounded liability that have limited the market's growth. For example, it must answer questions such as whether or not identity providers should have legal protection if they have complied with the defined standards and credentials are nonetheless issued or used incorrectly.

The Federal Government may need to establish or amend both policies and laws to address these concerns. Multiple entities currently enforce online security and privacy standards in a distributed fashion across both government and the private sector. Any new laws and policies must maintain the flexibility of this approach, while harmonizing a diverse and sometimes conflicting set of requirements that currently prevent interoperability and trust across communities.

Objective 1.4: Establish a steering group to administer the standards development and accreditation process for the Identity Ecosystem Framework.

The policy and technical standards necessary for the Identity Ecosystem may be developed in different fora. A steering group will thus administer the process for policy and technical standards development for the Identity Ecosystem Framework. The group will bring together all of the interested stakeholders to ensure that the Identity Ecosystem Framework provides a minimum baseline of privacy, security, and interoperability through standards, policies, and laws—without creating unnecessary barriers to entry. The steering group will work diligently to follow the Guiding Principles in this Strategy; it will organize and conduct itself in the spirit of those principles, as the inclusive, transparent, pragmatic, and committed leadership group building toward the Strategy's vision. To that end, the steering group will also set milestones and measure progress against them. The steering group will also ensure that accreditation authorities validate participants' adherence to the requirements of the Identity Ecosystem Framework.

Goal 2: Build and implement the Identity Ecosystem.

The Identity Ecosystem Framework includes the standards, policies, and laws that serve as a platform for the Identity Ecosystem; however, it is not the Ecosystem. The Identity Ecosystem must be built and implemented, primarily by the private sector, with interoperable identity solutions that are aligned with the Identity Ecosystem Framework.

Objective 2.1: Implement the private-sector elements of the Identity Ecosystem.

The Strategy can only succeed if the private sector voluntarily implements the Identity Ecosystem and only if it makes business sense to do so. The vast majority of the Identity Ecosystem will be built by the private sector, and almost all of the Identity Ecosystem's subjects, relying parties, identity providers, attribute providers, and accreditation authorities will be in the private sector.

The private sector is already providing many services that, if they choose, could be a part of the Identity Ecosystem. We encourage these providers to participate in the development of the Identity Ecosystem Framework and the implementation of the Identity Ecosystem, to ensure that both incorporate these providers' knowledge and experience.

To support the private sector, the Federal Government will work to promote and incentivize both innovation in the marketplace and the private sector's implementation of the Identity Ecosystem in accordance with the Identity Ecosystem Framework.

Objective 2.2: Implement the state, local, tribal, and territorial government elements of the Identity Ecosystem.

State, local, tribal, and territorial governments have a significant role in building the Identity Ecosystem. These levels of government may at times act as identity or attribute providers. They will also offer services online as relying parties and, as subjects, will use services provided by others.

These levels of government have a high level of interaction with their constituents, and they have a unique insight into the needs of individuals and local organizations. Their participation in the Identity Ecosystem will significantly increase the value that it provides to the Nation.

Similar to its efforts with the private sector, the Federal Government will promote and incentivize all levels of governments' implementation of the Identity Ecosystem in accordance with the Identity Ecosystem Framework.

Objective 2.3: Implement the Federal Government elements of the Identity Ecosystem.

The Federal Government will also implement the Identity Ecosystem. In the areas where it has unique capabilities, the Federal Government may act as an identity or attribute provider. It will also offer services online as a relying party and, as a subject, will use services provided by others.

The Federal Government must continue to lead by example and be an early adopter of identity solutions that align with the Identity Ecosystem Framework. By adopting Identity Ecosystem solutions as a service provider, the Federal Government will raise individual's expectations and thus drive individuals' demand for interoperability in their transactions with the private sector and other levels of government.

As a subject, the Federal Government must also continue to leverage its buying power as a significant customer of the private sector to motivate the supply of these solutions.

To that end, the expansion of government services, pilots, and policies that align with the Identity Ecosystem should be accelerated.[10] The Federal Government will continue to follow the *FICAM Roadmap and Implementation Guidance* and will build upon that work to further advance the Identity Ecosystem.

Objective 2.4: Promote the deployment of interoperable solutions to implement the Identity Ecosystem Framework.

The Federal Government must promote the implementation of interoperable solutions that support trusted identities for online transactions. The Federal Government will work with the private sector and all other levels of government to organize, coordinate, promote, and participate in pilot programs that are interoperable across sectors and that implement the Identity Ecosystem. The Federal Government will also seek to initiate and support pilots that address the needs of individuals, the private sector, and of all levels of government. Finally, the Federal Government will promote interoperability by sharing its existing and new infrastructure, such as test beds and approved products and services, with the other participants on the Identity Ecosystem. The private sector and all levels of government should share information on the lessons learned from these and other implementation efforts.

Goal 3: Enhance confidence and willingness to participate in the Identity Ecosystem.

The greater the number of participants in the Identity Ecosystem, the greater the value that each will obtain from participation. Individuals benefit when they can choose to use any single identity provider to access a large number of relying parties. Relying parties benefit when they can more easily access a wide pool of customers. The success of the Identity Ecosystem thus depends, in large part, on encouraging individuals and organizations to adopt it.

Objective 3.1: Provide awareness and education to enable informed decisions.

The public and private sector will use awareness and education programs to encourage demand for the Identity Ecosystem and to inform its use. Awareness efforts will help inform individuals and organizations about the security and privacy risks associated with existing, weak authentication mechanisms. These efforts will also communicate the benefits of the Identity Ecosystem to all of the potential participants, including individuals, relying parties, and potential identity and attribute providers.

Education programs will ensure that individuals know how to obtain and use Identity Ecosystem credentials. For service providers, education programs can provide information on implementing Identity Ecosystem solutions and abiding by Identity Ecosystem policies.

---

10. For example, Executive Order 13556, Controlled Unclassified Information, establishes an open and uniform program for managing information that requires safeguarding. Once implemented, this Executive Order will enable increased information sharing with appropriately credentialed subjects. http://www.whitehouse.gov/the-press-office/2010/11/04/executive-order-controlled-unclassified-information

Education and awareness is an important area in which the Federal Government can assist individuals, other levels of government, and the private sector. The Federal Government is already working to raise public awareness regarding cybersecurity, and these efforts should be leveraged to raise awareness of the Identity Ecosystem. The Federal Government will work with the private sector and other levels of government to develop education and awareness programs and to customize them for groups like individuals and small businesses, who have unique needs. The Federal Government will also work with the private sector to provide information to potential service providers, to communicate how they can participate in and benefit from the Identity Ecosystem.

Objective 3.2: Identify other means to drive widespread adoption of the Identity Ecosystem.

All levels of government can assist the private sector by helping to jumpstart the adoption of the Identity Ecosystem, ensuring that it becomes widespread enough to be self-sustaining. In order to provide this jumpstart, all levels of government should work with the private sector to help identify economic incentives to encourage private-sector adoption of the Identity Ecosystem. The Federal Government will also align identity solution requirements in existing programs against the Identity Ecosystem. Finally, the Federal Government will evaluate regulatory changes as necessary.

Goal 4: Ensure the long-term success and sustainability of the Identity Ecosystem.

Over the long term, the Identity Ecosystem should become a self-sustaining marketplace, but the public and private sector must continue to participate in its maintenance, technical evolution, international integration, and adherence to the Guiding Principles.

Objective 4.1: Drive innovation through aggressive science and technology (S&T) and research and development (R&D) efforts.

The Identity Ecosystem is composed of technology and policy that must evolve to accommodate:

- Rapid and unanticipated advances in technologies that continuously revolutionize what can be done, how it is done, and who can participate in cyberspace.[11]

- Continuous innovation in imaginative new services, resources, and capabilities that increase the value of cyberspace to all sectors of society.

- Ever increasing needs and expectations for cyberspace.

As these trends constantly reshape cyberspace, the Identity Ecosystem must be continuously improved, stretching to meet new needs, enable new opportunities, and address future cyberspace threats. This requires the Federal Government to work in partnership with the academic and private sectors, both domestic and international, on interdisciplinary S&T and R&D. We need sustained, strategic investments to continually improve the security, reliability, resilience, and trustworthiness of the identification, authentication, and authorization of entities in cyberspace. Moreover, these efforts should extend

---

11. Revolutionizing Science and Engineering Through Cyberinfrastructure: Report of the National Science Foundation Blue-Ribbon Advisory Panel on Cyberinfrastructure. January 2003. http://www.nsf.gov/od/oci/reports/atkins.pdf

beyond the technical to address issues like usability, privacy, incentives, and processes. The Federal Government will also continue to promote the transfer of government-sponsored S&T and R&D results to the private sector, to ensure that the Identity Ecosystem adopts and deploys the advances that emerge from this effort.

Objective 4.2: Integrate the Identity Ecosystem internationally.

Given the global nature of online commerce, the Identity Ecosystem cannot be isolated from internationally available online services and their identity solutions. Without compromising the guiding principles of the Strategy, the public and private sectors will strive to enable international interoperability. In order for the U.S. to benefit from other nations' best practices and achieve international interoperability, the U.S. public and private sectors must be active participants in international technical and policy standardization fora.

No single entity, including the Federal Government, can effectively participate in every international standards effort. The private sector is already involved in many international standards initiatives; ultimately, then, the international integration of the Identity Ecosystem will depend in great part upon private-sector leadership. To better support the private sector, the Federal Government will increase its prioritization, coordination, and participation in relevant international technical and policy fora.

Commitment to Action

The implementation of the Identity Ecosystem will require the collaboration and joint commitment of both the public and private sectors. This section identifies, first, the respective roles of the public and private sectors and, second, the Federal Government implementation activities that are critical to building and maintaining the Identity Ecosystem.

Role of the Private Sector

Only the private sector has the ability to build and operate the complete Identity Ecosystem, and the final success of the Strategy depends upon private-sector leadership and innovation.

The key operational roles within the Identity Ecosystem include: subjects, relying parties, identity providers, attribute providers, and accreditation authorities. For each of these ecosystem roles, the private sector will constitute the majority of the actors. For example, most identity and attribute providers will be private-sector organizations.

The Strategy can only succeed if the Identity Ecosystem is self-sustaining, which will require the development of business models for each of the service provider roles in the ecosystem. Many of these business models will be entirely new, and only the private sector can provide the innovation necessary to realize them.

The private sector must also play a leadership role in the design and operation of the Identity Ecosystem. The development of the Identity Ecosystem Framework and the ongoing work to maintain accountability to that framework will require a true public-private partnership. The private sector has the insight into the needs of the market that is necessary to develop effective technical and policy standards for the Identity Ecosystem. For-profit organizations can help ensure that the Identity Ecosystem Framework provides sustainable business models and is not an onerous burden on the private sector. Advocacy groups and non-profits can magnify the voices of individuals and under-represented groups, and they can work to ensure the enhancement of privacy and to otherwise support civil liberties.

Role of the Federal Government

The Federal Government's role is to:

- Advocate for and protect individuals;
- Support the private sector's development and adoption of the Identity Ecosystem;
- Partner with the private sector to ensure that the Identity Ecosystem is sufficiently interoperable, secure, and privacy protecting;
- Provide and accept Identity Ecosystem services for which it is uniquely suited; and
- Lead by example and implement the Identity Ecosystem for the services it provides internally and externally.

The Federal Government will support the private sector's development and adoption of the Identity Ecosystem through activities such as: convening technology and policy standardization workshops, building consensus, establishing public policy frameworks, participating in international fora, funding research, supporting pilots, and initiating education and awareness efforts.

The Federal Government will partner with the private sector and participate in the development of the Identity Ecosystem Framework to ensure that it establishes a sufficient baseline of interoperability, security, and privacy. The Federal Government's role in this area is to help ensure the outcome; the private sector is better suited to ascertaining the means of achieving that outcome. This participation will also enable the Federal Government to advocate for and protect individuals. Among the actions that the Federal Government must undertake, privacy is the most important for individuals; as such the Federal Government will ensure that the FIPPs are effectively incorporated into the Identity Ecosystem Framework.

---

8. Envision It!

Ali wishes to fill his medical prescription online. He authenticates to an online pharmacy using a small plastic token that he stores on his keychain. Ali submits his request for the pharmacy to fill his prescription on their secure website.

Ali's attribute provider provides authoritative proof that he is over 18 and that his prescription is valid. Since the website and attribute provider are trustmarked and use privacy-enhancing technology, no unnecessary information is exchanged in this transaction. The pharmacy is not told Ali's birth date or the reason for the prescription. The technology also filters information so that the attribute providers—the authoritative sources of the age and prescription information—do not know what pharmacy Ali is using.

Ali is able to quickly and easily fill his prescription online. The privacy protections are conveniently built into the Identity Ecosystem, so Ali receives those protections automatically.

The Federal Government has a wealth of information that can be useful to the private sector, but this information can be scattered amongst different agencies and difficult to find. To better enable the private sector, the Federal Government will share its best practices and lessons learned in a centralized, accessible way.

The Federal Government must continue to be a leader through its own participation in the Identity Ecosystem as both a subject and relying party. Whenever possible, the Federal Government will use existing private-sector Identity Ecosystem solutions rather than developing or operating its own. Moreover, it must not require levels of assurance that are excessive compared to the risk of a given transaction. Through these actions, the Federal Government will encourage the market toward trustworthy and interoperable identity solutions.

The National Program Office

The Secretary of Commerce will establish within the Department of Commerce (Commerce) an interagency office to be known as the National Program Office (NPO) that is charged, consistent with statutory authorities, with achieving the goals of the Strategy. The NPO will be responsible for coordinating the processes and activities of organizations that will implement the Strategy. Commerce will host this interagency function, because it is uniquely suited to work with the private sector—and with government at all levels—to bring the collective expertise of the nation to bear in implementing the Strategy.

The NPO will lead the day-to-day coordination of NSTIC activities, working closely with the Cybersecurity Coordinator in the White House. The National Program Office will:

- Promote private-sector involvement and engagement;
- Support interagency collaboration and coordinate interagency efforts associated with achieving programmatic goals;
- Build consensus on policy frameworks necessary to achieve the vision;
- Identify areas for the government to lead by example in developing and supporting the Identity Ecosystem, particularly in the Executive Branch's role as a provider and validator of key credentials;
- Actively participate within and across relevant public- and private-sector fora; and
- Assess progress against the goals, objectives, and milestones of the Strategy and the associated implementation activities.

The NPO will actively seek interagency collaboration, partner with the private sector and individuals as necessary, harness multi-disciplinary and multi-sector contributions, and provide leadership across the Federal Government. In addition to the NPO, the President will designate agencies as leads and partners with the private sector for individual tasks to fulfill the goals and objectives of this Strategy.

Role of State, Local, Tribal, and Territorial Governments

Individuals interact with their State, local, tribal, and territorial governments as much or more than with the Federal Government. The Identity Ecosystem can help these governments decrease their costs, even as they increase the services they offer their constituents online.

Much like the Federal Government, these governments are well-positioned to lead efforts to protect individuals, help standardize policies, and act as early adopters in the provision and consumption of Identity Ecosystem services. As such, State, local, tribal, and territorial governments are encouraged to align with the Identity Ecosystem Framework and to support its establishment by participating in its development. As a first step, these governments are encouraged to align their efforts with existing Federal work like the *FICAM Roadmap and Implementation Guidance*.

One unique strength of these governments is their more direct and personal engagement with their constituents. The Federal Government will thus encourage them to initiate education and awareness efforts to engage individuals, small and local businesses, and other local organizations.

Role of International Partners

Other nations seek to supply their constituents with the benefits of more trusted identities online, and many are more advanced in their efforts than the United States. The public- and private-sectors' engagement with international partners will be critical to the success of the Identity Ecosystem: the long-term success of the Identity Ecosystem depends upon its international interoperability.

The Federal Government will thus seek to support the private sector's engagement in international fora and to improve its own direct engagement in these fora. The U.S. approach differs from that of many nations, who have or are pursuing national offline and online identities. The Federal Government explicitly rejects that approach for its own citizens but will work to help the private sector achieve interoperability with the policy and technical standards of other nations.

Implementation Roadmap and Federal Government Actions

Given its role as an enabler of the Identity Ecosystem, the Federal Government must organize quickly and prepare for the substantial public-private collaboration required to realize the Strategy's vision. As such, the Federal Government will develop an Implementation Roadmap that identifies and assigns responsibility for near- and long-term actions that the Federal Government can perform. These activities will leverage existing investments, standards, and best practices from the public and private sector, both nationally and internationally.

The Roadmap will focus on activities that:

- Mobilize all relevant Federal Government stakeholders to develop and support the Identity Ecosystem;
- Leverage existing work in government to quickly implement near-term solutions aligned with the Strategy;
- Remove barriers associated with the private-sector development of the Identity Ecosystem;
- Ensure the protection of individuals in the Identity Ecosystem Framework; and
- Promote Federal alignment with the Strategy as both a service provider and a consumer of services provided by the private sector.

Benchmarks

The success of the Strategy and the establishment of the Identity Ecosystem can be assessed by critical benchmarks in the near and long term. The NPO is responsible for identifying and developing specific objective metrics related to these benchmarks.

Interim Benchmarks (3-5 years)

The interim benchmarks reflect that the standardization of policy and technology and the initial implementation of the Identity Ecosystem will not occur overnight. These benchmarks will mark the point at which the Identity Ecosystem reaches its initial operating capacity, within 3-5 years. The benchmarks incorporate critical aspects of the Identity Ecosystem, such as public- and private-sector collaboration, privacy protection, broad participation, and interoperability. In addition, these benchmarks can be used to assess whether both organizations and individuals have the opportunity to realize the benefits of the Identity Ecosystem in the short term.

- Subjects have the ability to choose trusted digital identities:
  - For personal or business use;
  - Between at least two identity credential and media types; and
  - That are usable across multiple sectors.
- There exists a growing marketplace of both trustmarked, private-sector identity providers at different levels of assurance and private-sector relying parties that accept trustmarked credentials at different levels of assurance. This relying party population is not confined to just one or two sectors.
- Trustmarked attribute providers are available to assert validated attributes. Services available include the ability to assert validated attributes without providing uniquely identifiable information.
- The number of enrolled identities in the Identity Ecosystem is growing at a significant rate, and the number of authentication transactions in the Identity Ecosystem is growing at least at the same rate.
- Building upon FICAM, all online Federal Executive Branch services are aligned appropriately with the Identity Ecosystem and, where appropriate, accept identities and credentials from at least one of the trustmarked private-sector identity providers.

All references to a trustmark indicate that the service provider complies with the overarching set of interoperability standards, risk models, privacy and liability policies, requirements, and accountability mechanisms of the Identity Ecosystem Framework.

Longer-term Benchmarks (10 years)

After 10 years, the primary benefits of the Identity Ecosystem should be realized and it should be fully available to those who choose to adopt it. The evolution of the Identity Ecosystem will continue long past this benchmark, but it must by this point be self-sustaining.

- All implementation actions are complete, and all required policies, processes, tools, and technologies are in place and continuing to evolve to support the Identity Ecosystem.
- A majority of relying parties are choosing to be part of the Identity Ecosystem.
- A majority of U.S. Internet users regularly engage in transactions verified through the Identity Ecosystem.
- A majority of online transactions are happening within the Identity Ecosystem.
- A sustainable market exists for Identity Ecosystem identity and attribute service providers.

Conclusion

Our economic, societal, and personal reliance on cyberspace will continue to grow in the years ahead, and with it our need to trust the identities of those with whom we interact online. The protection of the identities of individuals and organizations while conducting online transactions is pivotal to protecting open commerce, promoting innovation, and securing our Nation. This Strategy proposes an Identity Ecosystem that will encourage trusted online transactions, provide privacy enhancements and support civil liberties, and reduce fraud.

Ultimately, the Identity Ecosystem can only be designed and built by the private sector. The Federal Government will support the private sector, ensure that the Identity Ecosystem respects the privacy and otherwise supports the civil liberties of individuals, and be a leader in implementing the Identity Ecosystem in its own services. Existing efforts by the public and private sectors have already established services that are significant components of the Identity Ecosystem, but much remains to be done. Individuals, businesses, non-profits, advocacy groups, associations, and all levels of government must work in partnership to improve how identities are trusted and used in cyberspace.

There is a compelling need to address these problems as soon as possible, making progress in the short-term and planning for the long-term. Through a collaborative effort by the public and private sectors, we can realize the vision and benefits of this Strategy and thus create a more secure cyberspace for our Nation.

Appendix A – Fair Information Practice Principles (FIPPs)

The Fair Information Practice Principles

To truly enhance privacy in the conduct of online transactions, the Fair Information Practice Principles (FIPPs) must be universally and consistently adopted and applied in the Identity Ecosystem. The FIPPs are the widely accepted framework of defining principles to be used in the evaluation and consideration of systems, processes, or programs that affect individual privacy.[12]

In brief, the Fair Information Practice Principles are:

- **Transparency:** Organizations should be transparent and notify individuals regarding collection, use, dissemination, and maintenance of personally identifiable information (PII).

- **Individual Participation:** Organizations should involve the individual in the process of using PII and, to the extent practicable, seek individual consent for the collection, use, dissemination, and maintenance of PII. Organizations should also provide mechanisms for appropriate access, correction, and redress regarding use of PII.

- **Purpose Specification:** Organizations should specifically articulate the authority that permits the collection of PII and specifically articulate the purpose or purposes for which the PII is intended to be used.

- **Data Minimization:** Organizations should only collect PII that is directly relevant and necessary to accomplish the specified purpose(s) and only retain PII for as long as is necessary to fulfill the specified purpose(s).

- **Use Limitation:** Organizations should use PII solely for the purpose(s) specified in the notice. Sharing PII should be for a purpose compatible with the purpose for which the PII was collected.

- **Data Quality and Integrity:** Organizations should, to the extent practicable, ensure that PII is accurate, relevant, timely, and complete.

- **Security:** Organizations should protect PII (in all media) through appropriate security safeguards against risks such as loss, unauthorized access or use, destruction, modification, or unintended or inappropriate disclosure.

- **Accountability and Auditing:** Organizations should be accountable for complying with these principles, providing training to all employees and contractors who use PII, and auditing the actual use of PII to demonstrate compliance with these principles and all applicable privacy protection requirements.

Universal application of the FIPPs provides the basis for confidence and trust in online transactions.

---

12. Rooted in the United States Department of Health, Education and Welfare's seminal 1973 report, "Records, Computers and the Rights of Citizens" (1973), these principles are at the core of the Privacy Act of 1974 and are mirrored in the laws of many U.S. states, as well as in those of many foreign nations and international organizations. A number of private and not-for-profit organizations have also incorporated these principles into their privacy policies. See, also guidance at http://www.dhs.gov/xlibrary/assets/privacy/privacy_policyguide_2008-01.pdf.

www.ingramcontent.com/pod-product-compliance
Lightning Source LLC
LaVergne TN
LVHW060148070326
832902LV00018B/3013